Upper Columbia Basin Network Aspen Monitoring Annual Report 2009

City of Rocks National Reserve (CIRO)

Natural Resource Technical Report NPS/UCBN/NRTR—2010/386

Eva K. Strand, Ph.D.
Department of Rangeland Ecology and Management
University of Idaho
Moscow, Idaho 83844-1135

Stephen C. Bunting, Ph.D
Department of Rangeland Ecology and Management
University of Idaho
Moscow, Idaho 83844-1135

October 2010

U.S. Department of the Interior
National Park Service
Natural Resource Program Center
Fort Collins, Colorado

The National Park Service, Natural Resource Program Center publishes a range of reports that address natural resource topics of interest and applicability to a broad audience in the National Park Service and others in natural resource management, including scientists, conservation and environmental constituencies, and the public.

The Natural Resource Technical Report Series is used to disseminate results of scientific studies in the physical, biological, and social sciences for both the advancement of science and the achievement of the National Park Service mission. The series provides contributors with a forum for displaying comprehensive data that are often deleted from journals because of page limitations.

All manuscripts in the series receive the appropriate level of peer review to ensure that the information is scientifically credible, technically accurate, appropriately written for the intended audience, and designed and published in a professional manner. Data in this report were collected and analyzed using methods based on established, peer-reviewed protocols and were analyzed and interpreted within the guidelines of the protocols.

Views, statements, findings, conclusions, recommendations, and data in this report do not necessarily reflect views and policies of the National Park Service, U.S. Department of the Interior. Mention of trade names or commercial products does not constitute endorsement or recommendation for use by the U.S. Government.

This report is also available from the Upper Columbia Basin Network (http://www.nature.nps.gov/im/units/UCBN) and the Natural Resource Publication Management website (http://www.nature.nps.gov/publications/NRPM) on the internet.

Please cite this publication as:

Strand, E. K., and S. C. Bunting. 2010. Upper Columbia Basin Network aspen monitoring annual report 2009: City of Rocks National Reserve (CIRO). Natural Resource Technical Report NPS/UCBN/NRTR—2010/386. National Park Service, Fort Collins, Colorado.

NPS 003/105822, October 2010

Contents

Figures

Tables

Appendices

Executive Summary

The mission of the National Park Service is "to conserve unimpaired the natural and cultural resources and values of the national park system for the enjoyment of this and future generations (NPS 1999). To uphold this goal, the Director of the NPS approved the Natural Resource Challenge to encourage national parks to focus on the preservation of the nation's natural heritage through science, natural resource inventories, and expanded resource monitoring (NPS 1999). Through the Challenge, 270 parks in the national park system were organized into 32 inventory and monitoring networks.

The Upper Columbia Basin Network has identified 14 priority vital signs, indicators of ecosystem health, which represent a broad suite of ecological phenomena operating across multiple temporal and spatial scales. Our intent has been to monitor a balanced and integrated suite of vital signs that meets the needs of current park management, but will also be able to accommodate unanticipated environmental conditions in the future. Quaking aspen is one particularly high priority vital sign for two UCBN parks, City of Rocks National Reserve (CIRO) and Craters of the Moon National Monument and Preserve (CRMO). Aspen is a focal resource at CIRO and CRMO because of its biological and aesthetic significance. Aspen clones are among the most biologically rich plant communities in the Intermountain West and act as a keystone species. Although aspen comprise only a small percentage of the land cover in the parks, the community type contributes significantly to species diversity and richness. Current observations of aspen decline and die-off in the western states are of concern to natural resource managers and scientists. Declining aspen habitats may cause losses of vertebrate species and vascular plants as well as invertebrates and nonvascular organisms. Aspen stands provide forage for grazers and browsers in western landscapes and declines in aspen may require adjustments in animal stocking rates. Aspen is an important attraction for campers, naturalists, and recreationists in the otherwise semi-arid landscapes of City of Rocks National Reserve and Craters of the Moon National Monument and Preserve.

The sampling design for aspen is divided into three sampling panels. Panel 1, consisting of 108 plots in 22 stands in CRMO, that was sampled in 2007. Panel 2, consisting of 86 plots in 16 stands in CIRO, was sampled in 2008. This annual report details the status estimates obtained during the third year of monitoring panel 3 during the field season 2009 in CIRO where 45 plots were sampled in 8 stands. Summary data from 2008 is also included in this report to provide a summary of the park data for CIRO. In addition, we detected an error in the calculation of aspen and conifer density in the annual report of 2008 (Strand and Bunting 2009), another reason to include corrected 2008 data in this annual report focusing on 2009.

In CRMO 34 stands were mapped in 2006 and 108 permanent plots were established in 22 stands in 2007. In CIRO, 67 aspen stands were mapped in 2006 using remote sensing and field reconnaissance. Of these, 37 stands were visited in 2008 and 86 permanent plots were established in 16 of the stands. In 2009 the remaining 30 stands were visited and 45 plots were established in 8 stands. Two additional stands in CIRO (stand #13 and #50) should have been sampled in 2009 but was thought to be located on private land. Stand #13 and #50 will be added to panel 3 next time this panel is sampled, which is planned for year 2012. The remaining 12 stands visited in CRMO and 41 stands visited in CIRO were either a different cover type than aspen (i.e. a mistake in vegetation mapping) or they were deemed unsuitable for sampling due to pre-determined criteria. In this protocol we limit sampling to upland aspen stands, excluding those in the riparian zone and shrubby snow-damaged aspen. A few stands were not feasible to sample because aspen occurred in ravines and on cliffs where transects and plots could not be placed for logistic and safety reasons. The park stem count averages (stems per hectare) for the 2008 and 2009 sampling effort in CIRO are shown in the table below.

Park	Year	Suckers[1]	Regeneration[2]	Mature[3]	Dead[4]
CIRO 1	2008	2,651	1,865	467	208
CIRO 2	2009	2,653	2,745	323	456
CIRO Total	2008-2009	2,652	2,167	418	293

[1] Suckers include suckers or seedlings < 5 feet tall. A sucker is an aspen shoot originating from vegetative sprouting from another aspen tree.
[2] Regeneration includes trees greater than 2.5 cm (1 inch) in diameter breast height (dbh) and shorter than 75% of the stand height.
[3] Mature trees are greater than 2.5 cm (1 inch) in dbh and taller than 75% of the stand height.
[4] Dead stems are greater than 2.5 cm (1 inch) in dbh.

The majority of the aspen stands sampled in CIRO in 2008-2009 are regenerating and contain a distribution of age classes. There are some stands, however, with relatively low aspen stem densities, low regeneration, and/or high dead aspen stem and conifer densities. Stand #24 has a low regeneration stem count of 159 stems/ha and also a relatively low suckering level, 637 stems/ha. Four stands have a dead stem count over 500 stems/ha, namely stand #7 (771 stems/ha), stand #11 (547 stems/ha), stand #61 (796 stems/ha) and stand #73 (895 stems/ha). In CIRO, 15 of the sampled stands contain conifer stems at low levels, of those, 7 stands contain mature conifer trees. Stands #37 and #40 contained a conifer stem density similar to the aspen stem density.

The aspen protocol was approved in September 2009. The methods presented in this report reflect that version, version 1.0 of the protocol. The power analysis is being refined to optimize the number of samples necessary for detecting trend with statistical confidence while minimizing the sampling efforts and costs. This is the last year of initial data collection, assessment, and establishment of permanent plots. In future years, the focus for data analysis will shift toward trend analysis, in which biologically meaningful declines or increases within the park units as well as within individual stands will be reported, providing ecological decision support information and enabling development of appropriate management strategies.

Acknowledgements

Funding for this project was provided through the National Park Service Natural Resource Challenge and the Servicewide Inventory and Monitoring Program. We thank the Oregon Museum of Science and Industry and members of its 2008 Salmon Camp program for field assistance. We thank the staff at City of Rocks National Reserve and Craters of the Moon National Monument and Preserve for contributions and critique of the aspen monitoring protocol and for assistance during field reconnaissance. Sincere thanks to Kathryn Irvine and Leigh Ann Harrod for providing invaluable statistical expertise. We further thank Gina Wilson for the initial mapping of the City of Rocks National Reserve vegetation.

Introduction

Aspen Ecology and Rationale for Monitoring

Quaking aspen (*Populus tremuloides*) is a member of the willow (*Salicaceae*) family and is the most widespread deciduous tree in North America (Little 1971). Although the geographic range is large, aspen's high evapotranspiration demands limit the species to areas where the annual precipitation exceeds 400 mm (DeByle 1985).

The life cycle of quaking aspen in the West is unique. Although aspen is a prolific producer of viable seed, conditions required for successful germination and establishment of aspen are rare in the West (Kemperman and Barnes 1976; Romme 1982; Mitton and Grant 1996). Many botanists argue that significant sexual reproduction in aspen has not occurred in the western United States within the last 10,000 years, since the last glacial retreat (Einspahr and Winton 1976; McDonough 1985). An example of recent successful establishments of aspen seedlings followed the severe fires in Yellowstone in 1988, which apparently provided a 'window of opportunity' of suitable substrate and climate conditions (Romme et al. 2005). The primary means of aspen reproduction in the West is via vegetative root suckering (Bartos 2001). While limited vegetative reproduction occurs within many established stands, prolific vegetative reproduction in aspen clones requires disturbance to promote suckering. Mortality of individual aspen stems caused by disturbance interrupts the balance between the two hormones auxin and cytokinin such that when mature aspen trees are killed or stressed the flow of auxin is suppressed and cytokinin can begin to stimulate root suckering (Bartos 2001). According to Barnes (1975) aspen clones can exist as self-regenerating organisms for thousands of years through periodic disturbance. Although aspen clones are long-lived, individual aspen stems are short-lived, normally living 100-150 years (Shepperd et al. 2001) with some occasionally exceeding 200 years (Mueggler 1989). Since sexual regeneration requires prolonged moist conditions and is extremely rare for intermountain western aspen, an aspen clone lost from the landscape will generally not regenerate from seed (Mitton and Grant 1996).

Aspen stands in the western mountains commonly occur in conjunction with conifer species but have also been observed as uneven-aged aspen stands where aspen appears to persist as a stable, self-regenerating ecosystem. These stable aspen systems are unsuitable for conifers or are far away from conifer seed sources (Mueggler 1989). In biophysical settings where aspen is seral to conifer species, slow-growing shade tolerant conifers begin to overtop aspen late in succession and will eventually outcompete and lead to aspen loss (Shepperd et al. 2001). Shepperd et al. (2001) show that aspen growth rates are independent of the presence of conifers in early to mid-succession and estimate that conifers will begin to out-compete aspen at a stand age of 100-150 years.

Browsing by wildlife and livestock has been shown to inhibit successful regeneration in aspen stands (Bartos and Campbell 1998; Kay and Bartos 2000; Kaye et al. 2005). Aspen regeneration is particularly affected within elk (*Cervus elaphus*) winter range in areas when elk populations are high and where elk are not hunted (Hart and Hart 2001). Recent research (Kaye et al. 2005) confirms that high levels of elk browsing and conifer dominance negatively influence aspen establishment but do not affect the growth or mortality of individual mature aspen ramets.

Drought within the past decade has been reported to cause mortality in aspen in Colorado (Worrall et al. 2008) and in the Canadian parklands (Brandt et al. 2003; Frey et al. 2004). In Colorado, mature stands on south-facing slopes at low elevation were found to be particularly susceptible to disease and insects as a result of acute drought and high temperatures. Aspen dieback in Canada has been correlated to factors such as stand age, drought and freeze-thaw events, defoliation, wood-boring insects, and fungal pathogens (Brandt et al. 2003; Frey et al. 2004). Rising temperatures and drought have also been correlated with increased forest mortality in the southwestern U.S. (van Mantgem and Stephenson 2007; van Mantgem et. al. 2009).

A recent phenomenon affecting western aspen is referred to as 'aspen die-off' and is different from the slow decline in aspen populations that has been occurring over the past century. In cases of 'aspen die-off' mature aspen stems are dying with no apparent regeneration in the form of suckering (http://www.fs.fed.us/rmrs/docs/congressional-briefing/issues/aspen-die-off.pdf). Scientists and managers are currently researching the causes and trying to find solutions to this die-off, currently affecting as much as 10% of western aspen stands (http://spectre.nmsu.edu/dept/docs/forest/AspenDieOff.pdf).

Aspen is an important resource to City of Rocks National Reserve (CIRO) and Craters of the Moon National Monument and Preserve (CRMO) because of its biological and aesthetic significance. Although aspen comprise only a small percentage of the land cover in the parks, the community type contributes significantly to species diversity and richness (Shive and Peterson 2001; Madison et al. 2003). Aspen brings visitors to the western mountains and parks, improves local economies, inspires poets and artists, and is portrayed in modern stories as well as tribal myths (McCool 2001). Aspen is an important attraction for campers, naturalists, and recreationists in the otherwise semi-arid landscapes of CIRO and CRMO.

The Upper Columbia Basin Network has identified 14 priority vital signs to monitor. Aspen exhibits a relatively slow range of change compared to other vital signs chosen and covers a greater spatial extent in the two parks where it is monitored. Information gained from monitoring aspen will contribute to the weight of ecological knowledge about natural resources at CIRO and CRMO and to regional management strategies for the conservation of aspen. In particular, aspen in CIRO and CRMO occur in areas that are near or below the precipitation threshold of 400 mm per year (Perala 1990) where upland aspen can persist long-term. Aspen in these parks may be one of the first species to respond to locally changing climate, and the response may be a decline in regeneration or a die-off of older clones. It is not currently known how aspen will react to a changing climate, and the trends observed, as part of this monitoring protocol, may contribute valuable data to future aspen management in the western United States.

Objectives

The overarching programmatic goal of the UCBN aspen vital signs monitoring program is to obtain data that will inform management decisions pertaining to the perpetuation of quaking aspen populations at CIRO and CRMO. The monitoring protocol addresses the following specific measurable monitoring objectives:

- Estimate current status and long-term trend in regeneration of park aspen populations as well as individual stands.
- Estimate status and trend in aspen abundance, as measured by stem density of live and dead trees, within aspen stands. Specifically, live aspen stems will be counted in five size classes: Class I - Suckers or seedlings < 46 cm (1.5 ft) tall, Class II - Suckers or seedlings 46 - 152 cm (1.5-5 ft) tall, Class III - Greater than 152 cm (5 ft) and up to 2.5 cm (1 inch) in diameter at breast height (dbh), Class IV - Greater than 152 cm (5 ft) and > 2.5 cm (1 inch) in diameter at breast height (dbh) but < 75% of the stand height, Class V - Greater than 2.5 cm (1 inch) in dbh and > 75% of the stand height.
- Estimate the status and trend in dead standing aspen stems.
- Estimate the status and trend of conifer density within aspen stands.

The following statistical sampling objectives have been developed for this protocol:

- Estimate with 90% confidence the mean, $\hat{\mu}$, within $\pm$ 25% of the true mean, μ, for aspen stem density (stems/ha) of suckers (class I+II), regeneration (class III+IV), mature trees (class V) and dead stems within aspen clones.
- Detect with >80% certainty (power, or 1-β) a change $\geq$ 25% between any two sequential time periods (5 years) of mean aspen live or dead stem density estimates with a 0.10 acceptable false-change (α) error rate. All upland aspen stands, larger than 0.3 ha in size, that are not located in entirely in riparian areas or composed of shrubby snow-damaged aspen will be sampled.

Methods

Sampling methods followed those detailed by Strand et al. (2009). All aspen stands available for sampling were classified via remote sensing, delineated on aerial photos or using a Global Positioning System unit (GPS) in the field in the City of Rocks National Reserve (Figure 1) in 2006. According to the protocol revisit design (Table 1) panel 1 in CRMO was sampled in 2007, and panel 2, the first set of sampling units in CIRO, was sampled in 2008 and panel 3, the second set of sampling units in CIRO, was sampled in 2009. The sampling units organizes the aspen stands in groups that are geographically close, and helps field crews focus on certain areas with common access roads or trails. Once initial baseline data is collected over 2 time periods (2007-2009) and (2010-2012) for each stand, sampling will continue on a 5-year cycle.

Table 1. Proposed revisit design for CRMO and CIRO. The first two sampling sessions will follow a [1-2] revisit design. Subsequent sampling sessions will follow a [1-4] revisit design in which one panel is located in CRMO and two panels are located in CIRO.

Panel	Sampling Occasion (Year)										
	2007	2008	2009	2010	2011	2012	2013	2014	2015	2016	2017
1 - CRMO	X			X					X		
2 - CIRO1		X			X					X	
3 - CIRO2			X			X					X

Permanent sampling transects were established within aspen stands. The number of transects established in each stand was determined by completing a power analysis that allowed for detection of trend with statistical confidence (0.90) and power (0.80) while minimizing the sampling effort. The number of transects placed in each stand was further weighted by the area of the stand such that more transects were placed in larger stands. The starting point for each transect was randomly located within the stand boundary and transects were oriented north-south or east-west depending on the orientation of the stand. Four plots were placed along each transect with a distance of 25 m between plot centers. Based on a variogram analysis, plots that are at least 25 m apart are considered to be spatially independent (Strand et al. 2009). The number of transects within each aspen stand was determined via the power analysis and then weighted by the areal extent of the stand. Altogether 86 plots were placed within 16 stands in the first sampling panel in CIRO in 2008 and 45 plots were established in 8 stands in 2009 (Figure 1). Maps of the stands sampled in 2009, including plot locations, are shown in Figure 2-5. Among all mapped stands within the parks, 12 stands in CRMO and 41 stands in CIRO were deemed unsuitable for sampling (Table 2) because of predetermined criteria (size, predominantly riparian vegetation, extensive snow-damage, or unsafe to sample). The GIS database of aspen stands describes which stands are sampled and the reason for not sampling other stands. In some cases there was no aspen in the area classified as an aspen stand using remote sensing in 2006. These stands usually contained broadleaf shrubby vegetation (e.g. *Prunus* spp.) or curl-leaf mountain-mahogany (*Cercocarpus ledifolius*). These 10 stands were removed from the aspen GIS database for CIRO because the stands did not contain aspen. The GIS database for CIRO currently contains 57 stands of which 26 are eligible for sampling.

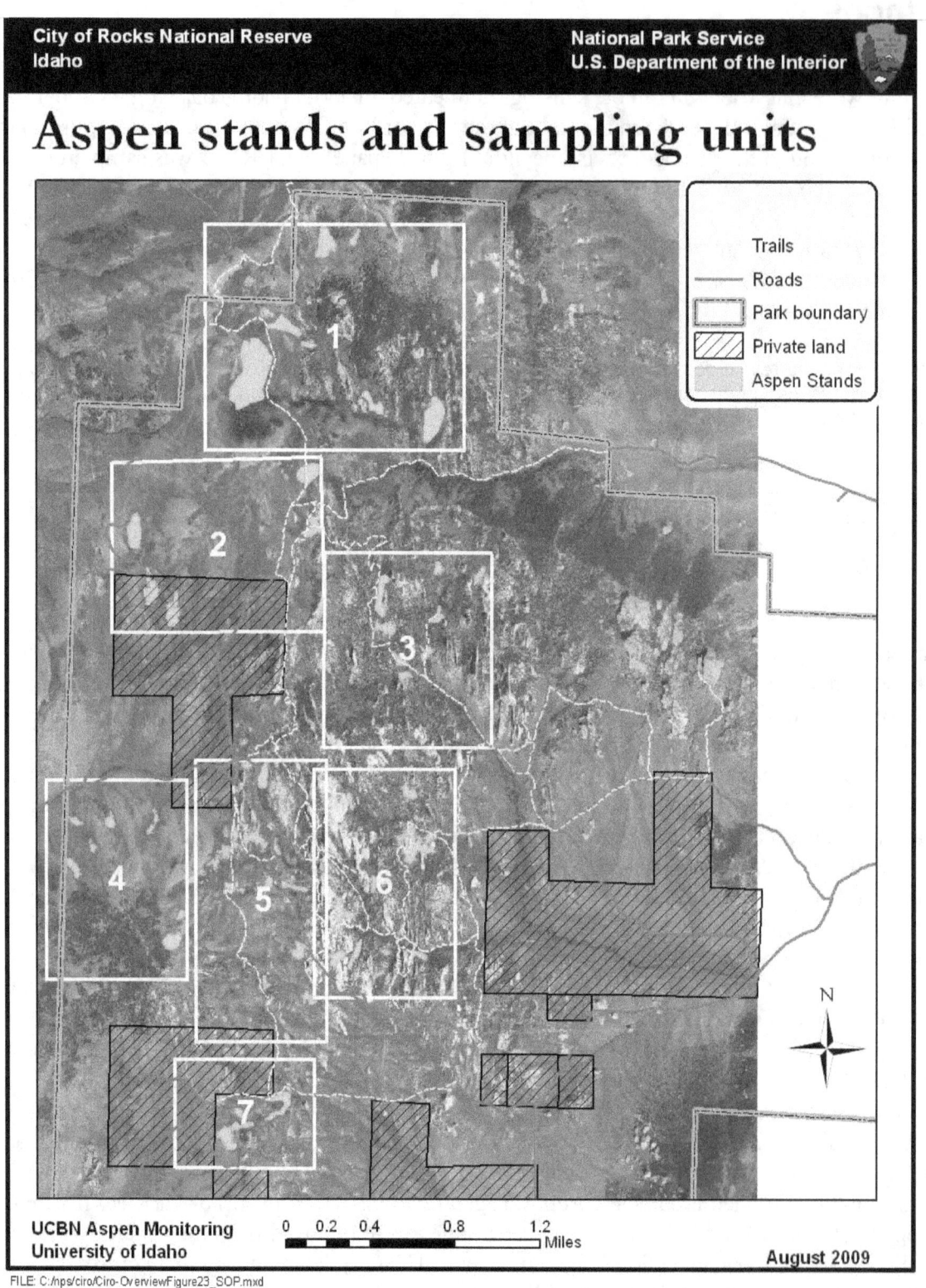

Figure 1. Map of aspen stands in CIRO divided into seven sampling units. The sampling units organizes the aspen stands in groups that are geographically close, and helps field crews focus on certain areas with common access roads or trails.

Table 2. The number of mapped stands within sampling units in CIRO, including the number of stands that were selected for long-term monitoring.

Unit	# mapped stands	Year visited	# selected for sampling	# unsuitable for sampling
1	9	2008-09	4	5
2	5	2009	3	2
3	9	2009	1	8
4	7	2008	2	5
5	12	2008	11	1
6	10	2008	1	9
7	5	2009	4	1

The numbers of aspen and conifer stems within pre-determined size classes (Table 3) that were rooted or had at least 50% of the stem diameter at ground level rooted within the 4-m radius plot were counted. Conifer plants shorter than 15 cm above ground were not counted. Dead stems that were lying on the ground were not counted, however dead stems that were leaning or otherwise partially standing were counted, if they were rooted or had at least 50% of the stem diameter at ground level rooted in the plot.

Table 3. Size classes of aspen and conifers.

Class I	Suckers or seedlings < 46 cm (1.5 ft) tall. Conifer seedlings shorter than 15 cm (6 inches) are not counted due to uncertainty in survival
Class II	Suckers or seedlings < 46 - 152 cm (1.5-5 ft) tall
Class III	Greater than 152 cm (5 ft) and up to 2.5 cm (1 inch) in dbh (diameter at breast height)
Class IV	Greater than 2.5 cm (1 inch) in dbh and shorter than 75% of the stand height
Class V	Greater than 2.5 cm (1 inch) in dbh and taller than 75% of the stand height
Class VI	Dead stems > 2.5 cm (1 inch) in dbh

Aspen total stem density by size class was calculated for each stand by adding all individual aspen stems within the sampled area and then dividing by the total sampled area (sum of sampled area within stand). Summary statistics are reported for four combinations of size classes as follows: Suckers (Class I+II), Regeneration (Class III+IV), Mature trees (Class V) and Dead stems (Class VI).

A distance photo of each aspen stand was taken from a location with a good vantage point that overlooked the stand. The UTM coordinates, NAD83 datum, and true north azimuth in the direction the photo was oriented are recorded.

Figure 2. Aspen stands in sampling unit 1. Stand #5 and #6 were sampled in 2008. Stand #9 and #73 were sampled in 2009.

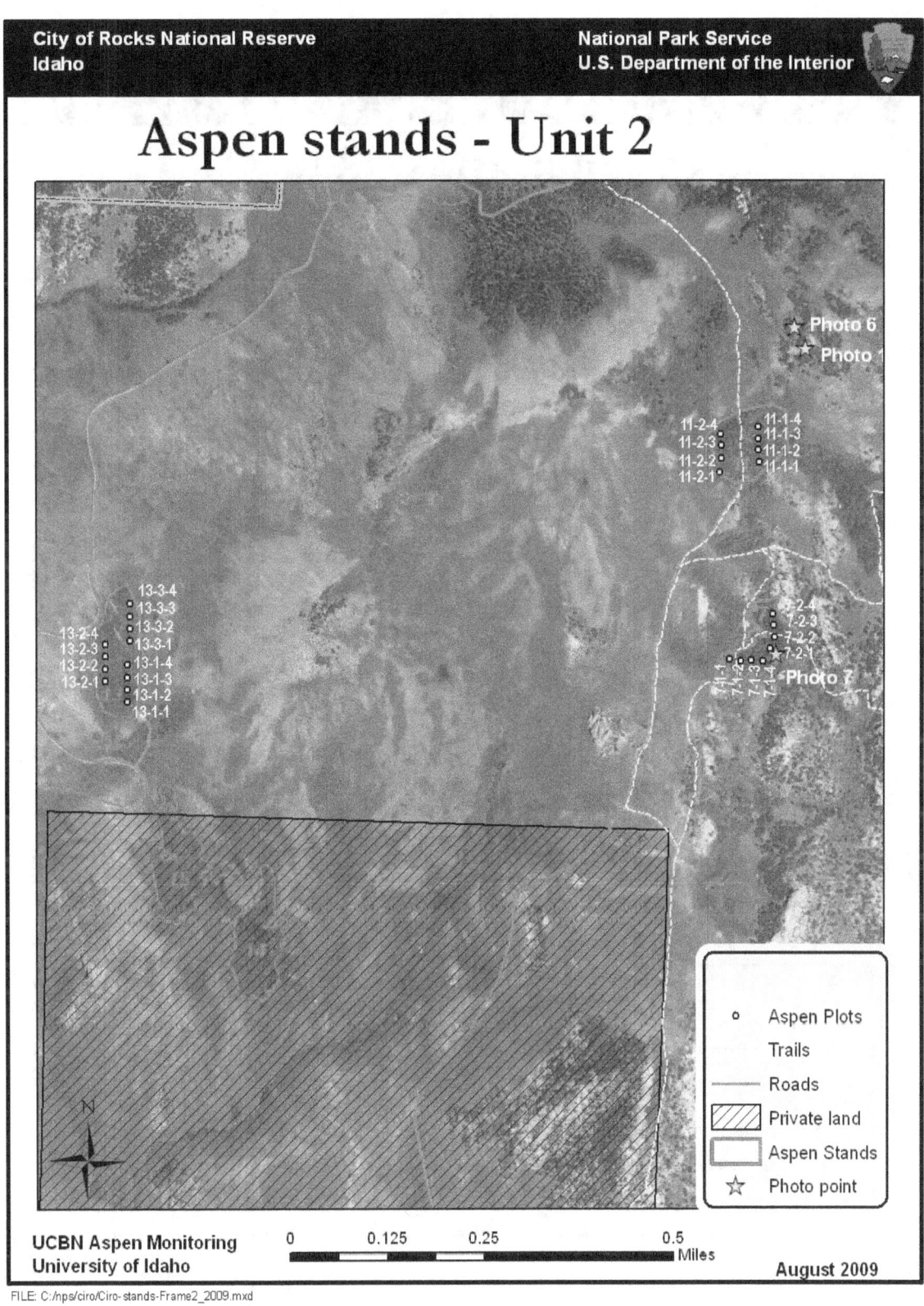

Aspen stands - Unit 2

Photo 6
Photo 1

11-2-4   11-1-4
11-2-3   11-1-3
11-2-2   11-1-2
11-2-1   11-1-1

13-3-4
13-3-3
13-3-2
13-2-4   13-3-1
13-2-3
13-2-2   13-1-4
13-2-1   13-1-3
13-1-2
13-1-1

7-2-4
7-2-3
7-2-2
7-2-1

Photo 7

	Legend
○	Aspen Plots
	Trails
	Roads
▨	Private land
▢	Aspen Stands
☆	Photo point

N

UCBN Aspen Monitoring
University of Idaho

0   0.125   0.25   0.5
Miles

August 2009

FILE: C:/nps/ciro/Ciro-stands-Frame2_2009.mxd

Figure 3. Aspen stands in sampling unit 2. Stand #7 and #11 were sampled in 2009. Stand #13 will be sampled next time this unit is sampled in 2012.

9

Figure 4. Aspen stands in sampling unit 3. Stand #24 was sampled in 2009.

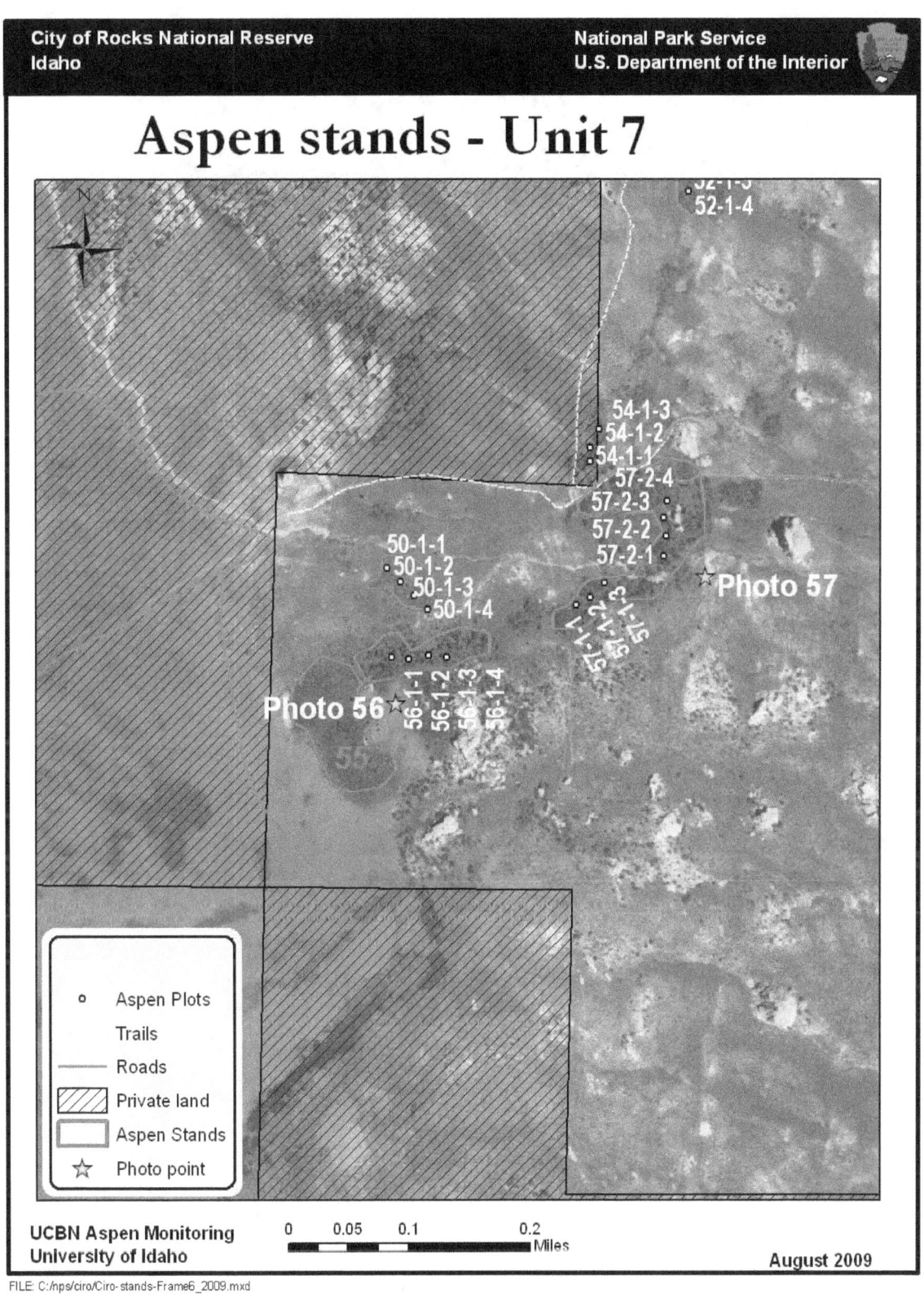

Aspen stands - Unit 7

52-1-4

54-1-3
54-1-2
54-1-1
57-2-4
57-2-3
57-2-2
57-2-1

50-1-1
50-1-2
50-1-3
50-1-4

Photo 57

Photo 56
56-1-1
56-1-2
56-1-3
56-1-4

55

Legend

○ Aspen Plots

Trails

Roads

Private land

Aspen Stands

☆ Photo point

UCBN Aspen Monitoring
University of Idaho

0   0.05   0.1   0.2
                              Miles

August 2009

FILE: C:/nps/ciro/Ciro-stands-Frame6_2009.mxd

Figure 5. Aspen stands in sampling unit 7. Stand #54, #56, and #57 were sampled in 2009. Stand #50 will be added to this sampling unit in 2012.

Results

During the 2009 field season, 30 stands were visited and 45 plots were established and sampled in 8 stands in the second sampling panel in CIRO (sampling units 1, 2, 3, and 7, Figure 2-5). There were several reasons why stands were not sampled. Stands #1, #2, #3, and #4 in unit 1 were composed of short shrubby snow-damaged aspen and stand #8 was located in a rocky ravine and the aspen stems were sparse and mixed with other broadleaf vegetation. In sampling unit 2, stands #14 and #15 were located on private land and were therefore not sampled. In sampling unit 3, stands #16, #18, #23, #26, and #27 were located in the riparian zone and mixed with other broadleaf vegetation. Stands #20 and #22 were located in rocky ravines where transects could not be placed for logistic and safety reasons. In sampling unit 7, all stands were selected for sampling except #55, which was a shrubby, snow-damaged stand. See Appendix A for a summary of all mapped aspen stands in CIRO, whether they are sampled or not and reasons for not sampling.

Aspen total stem density by size class was calculated for each stand by adding all individual aspen stems within the sampled area and then dividing by the total sampled area (sum of sampled area within stand). Summary statistics are reported in stems/ha for four combinations of size classes as follows: Suckers (Class I+II), Regeneration (Class III+IV), Mature trees (Class V) and Dead stems (Class VI) for CIRO during the sampling seasons 2008 and 2009 (Table 4) and by stand (Table 5).

Table 4. Park stem count averages for the 2008-2009 sampling effort.

Park	Year	Suckers	Regeneration	Mature	Dead
CIRO 1	2008	2,651	1,865	467	208
CIRO 2	2009	2,653	2,745	323	456
CIRO Total	2008-2009	2,652	2,167	418	293

[1] Suckers include suckers or seedlings < 5 feet tall. A sucker is an aspen shoot originating from vegetative sprouting from another aspen tree.
[2] Regeneration includes trees greater than 2.5 cm (1 inch) in diameter breast height (dbh) and shorter than 75% of the stand height.
[3] Mature trees are greater than 2.5 cm (1 inch) in dbh and taller than 75% of the stand height.
[4] Dead stems are greater than 2.5 cm (1 inch) in dbh.

In CIRO the lowest regeneration was observed in stand #24 (159 stems/ha), which also showed a low suckering level (637 stems/ha). Four stands had a dead stem count higher than 500 stems/ha, stand #7 (771 stems/ha), #11 (547 stems/ha), #61 (796 stems/ha) and #73 (895 stems/ha).

Conifers were present in 15 of the 24 sampled stands in CIRO in 2008-2009 (Table 6). Rocky mountain juniper (*Juniperus scopulorum*) was present in six stands (# 9, 37, 40, 41, 43, 45), Utah juniper *(Juniperus osteosperma)* was present in six stands (#9, 24, 30, 54, 56, 57), limber pine (*Pinus flexilis*) was present in two stands (#6 and 73), pinyon pine (*Pinus monophylla*) was present in four stands (# 24, 30, 37, 45), and Douglas-fir (*Pseudotsuga menziesii*) and lodgepole pine (*Pinus contorta*) was present in one stands (#6). Seven stands contained mature conifer stems (#30, 37, 40, 41, 43, 56, 73). In stand #37 and #40, the stem density of mature conifer stems was comparable to the stem density of mature aspen stems.

Table 5. Aspen stem counts by stand and the average number of stems per hectare in CIRO for sampling seasons 2008 and 2009.

Stand #	Suckers (stems/ha)	Regeneration (stems/ha)	Mature (stems/ha)	Dead (stems/ha)	Sampling year
5	2,670	1,449	654	114	2008
6	2,462	3,506	373	124	2008
7	1,616	3,855	174	771	2009
9	3,017	2,918	464	398	2009
11	1,393	2,537	448	547	2009
24	637	159	358	80	2009
30	3,233	2,586	597	99	2008
33	2,188	1,923	265	66	2008
37	5,123	2,934	298	149	2008
38	332	862	332	66	2008
40	1,512	1,592	159	80	2008
41	1,421	1,222	540	171	2008
42	2,984	2,122	619	486	2008
43	3,084	995	338	279	2008
45	4,526	2,537	448	50	2008
51	2,537	995	995	249	2008
52	2,934	2,487	696	249	2008
54	2,852	2,586	66	133	2009
56	2,437	2,586	199	298	2009
57	6,650	3,240	313	284	2009
61	5,836	1,790	663	796	2008
63	1,251	1,705	256	199	2008
72	1,741	1,194	348	0	2008
73	2,288	3,332	448	895	2009
Year 2008	2,651	1,865	467	208	2008
Year 2009	2,653	2,745	323	455	2009
Park 08-09 Stems/ha	2,652	2,167	418	293	

Table 6. Conifer density in sampled aspen stands at CIRO in 2008 and 2009.

Stand #	Suckers (stems/ha)	Regeneration (stems/ha)	Mature (stems/ha)	Dead (stems/ha)	Sampling year
5	0	0	0	85	2008
6	25	497	0	0	2008
7	0	0	0	0	2009
9	0	99	0	0	2009
11	0	0	0	0	2009
24	80	80	0	0	2009
30	0	50	50	0	2008
33	0	0	0	0	2008
37	50	199	298	50	2008
38	0	0	0	0	2008
40	0	119	159	40	2008
41	28	114	57	0	2008
42	0	0	0	0	2008
43	60	60	40	20	2008
45	99	99	0	0	2008
51	0	0	0	0	2008
52	0	0	0	0	2008
54	0	199	0	0	2009
56	99	49	49	0	2009
57	85	369	0	0	2009
61	0	0	0	0	2008
63	0	0	0	0	2008
72	99	50	0	0	2008
73	0	50	149	0	2009
Year 2008	23	88	42	14	2008
Year 2009	31	102	18	0	2009
Park 08-09 Stems/ha	26	93	33	9	

Discussion

Thresholds and management support

One of the goals of the aspen monitoring protocol is to suggest thresholds for when management action is needed for the long-term maintenance of aspen stands within CIRO and CRMO. In 2007 – 2009 we established permanent plots and sampled these parks for the first time. Further data quantifying the variation in stem counts through time is needed before we can begin to identify patterns, trends, and thresholds. Conditions identifying aspen stands at-risk have been suggested (Bartos and Campbell 1998) with the following specific thresholds:

> 1) aspen stands where the regeneration (stems 1.5-4.5 m tall) is < 1200 stems/ha
> 2) total aspen canopy cover is less than 40%
> 3) conifer canopy cover is greater than 25%
> 4) stands where the majority of the stems are greater than 100 years in age and decadent.

These thresholds were developed for aspen stands in Utah and Colorado and it is not certain if these thresholds are applicable to the aspen stands in CIRO and CRMO. Initial signs of aspen decline manifest themselves as reduced regeneration within the clone, decreasing number of aspen stems, and increasing counts of conifer stems and dead aspen stems. It is desirable to detect these initial signs of aspen decline at an early stage when management may more effectively reverse a negative trend. Monitoring aspen regeneration and density of live and dead stems and conifers is important for determining when active management could be considered for restoration and the long-term maintenance of aspen stands in the park. Data provided by this vital signs monitoring protocol will enable park managers to engage in adaptive and proactive management with the goal of long-term preservation of aspen habitats within the parks.

Stands of potential concern in CIRO

Although thresholds indicating when management action may be desirable for long-term maintenance of aspen stands at CIRO and CRMO have not been established, the following is a short summary describing stands with the lowest aspen stem densities, low regeneration, and high dead aspen stem and conifer densities for stands sampled in CIRO 2008-2009.

Stand #24: The suckering (637 stems/ha) and regeneration (159 stems/ha) was low in this stand (Figure 6). The mature stems density (358 stems/ha) was slightly below park average (418 stems/ha).

Stand #38: The suckering (332 stems/ha) and regeneration (862 stems/ha) was relatively low in this stand (Figure 7). The mature stems density (332 stems/ha) was below park average (418 stems/ha).

High counts of dead stems occurred in stand #7 (771 stems/ha), #11 (547 stems/ha), #61 (796 stems/ha) and #73 (895 stems/ha, Figure 8). These stands are located on hill slopes that are dependent on snow melt to provide moisture during the dry season. A warming climate trend resulting in earlier snow melt may effectively result in these aspen stands being subject to drought during the latter part of the growing season, when limited water availability could inhibit growth and recruitment. If this effect becomes great enough, these areas might cease to be suitable for aspen habitat. Determining the age of aspen stands that have a high dead stem count would be informative, since individual aspen stems are not expected to live much longer than 100 years before they die and leave room for regenerating stems. Stand age estimates could be accomplished using a nondestructive method such as taking cores using an increment borer. If stems are dying at a much younger age than 100 years, stressors are likely affecting the stand.

In stands #37 and #40, mature aspen and conifer densities were comparable. Conifers are present, and evidently regenerating in these stands, thus the stands may be at risk of conifer dominance and reduction in aspen density in the future.

Figure 6. The suckering (637 stems/ha) and regeneration (159 stems/ha) was low in stand #24. The mature stems density (358 stems/ha) was slightly below park average (418 stems/ha).

Figure 7. The suckering (332 stems/ha) and regeneration (862 stems/ha) was relatively low in stand #38. The mature stems density (332 stems/ha) was below park average (418 stems/ha).

Figure 8. High counts of dead stems occurred in stand #7 (771 stems/ha), #11 (547 stems/ha), #61 (796 stems/ha) and #73 (895 stems/ha)

Literature Cited

Barnes, B.V. 1975. Phenotypic variation of trembling aspen in Western North America. Forest Science 22:319-328.

Bartos, D.L. 2001. Landscape Dynamics of Aspen and Conifer Forests. p. 5-14. Sustaining Aspen in Western Landscapes: Symposium Proceedings; 13-15 June 2000; Grand Junction, CO. USDA Forest Service Proceedings RMRS-P-18.

Bartos, D.L., and R.B. Campbell. 1998. Decline of Quaking Aspen in the Interior West – Examples from Utah. Rangelands 20(1): 17-14.

Brandt, J.P., H.F. Cerzke, K.L. Mallett, W.J.A. Volney, and J.D. Weber. 2003. Factors affecting trembling aspen (*Populus tremuloides* Michx.) health in the boreal forest of Alberta, Saskatchewan, and Manitoba, Canada., Forest Ecology and Management 178:287-300.

DeByle N.V. 1985. Water and Watershed. p. 153-160, *in* DeByle and Winokur (Editors) Aspen: Ecology and Management in the Western United States. USDA Forest Service General Technical Report RM-119.

Einspahr D.W., L.L. Winton. 1976. Genetics of quaking aspen. USDAorest Service Research Paper WO-25. Washington (DC): USDA.

Frey, B.R., V.J. Lieffers, E.H. Hogg, and S.M. Landhäusser. 2004. Predicting landscape patterns of aspen dieback: mechanisms and knowledge gaps. Canadian Journal of Forest Research 34: 1379–1390.

Hart, J.H., and D.L. Hart. 2001. Interaction among cervids, fungi, and aspen in northwest Wyoming, p.197-205, Sustaining Aspen in Western Landscapes: Symposium Proceedings; 13-15 June 2000; Grand Junction, CO. USDA Forest Service Proceedings RMRS-P-18.

Kay, C.E. and D.L. Bartos. 2000. Ungulate herbivory on Utah aspen: Assessment of long term exclosures. Journal of Range Management 53:145-153.

Kaye, M.W., D. Binkley, and T.J. Stohlgren. 2005. Effects of conifers and elk browsing on quaking aspen forests in the central Rocky Mountains, USA. Ecological Applications 15:1284-1295.

Kemperman J.A., and B.V. Barnes. 1976. Clone size in American aspens. Canadian Journal of Botany 54:2603-2607.

Little, E.L., Jr. 1971. Atlas of United States trees: Vol. 1. Conifers and important hardwoods. U.S. Department of Agriculture, Forest Service, Miscellaneous Publications 1146, 9 p. 202 maps. Washington DC. http://climchange.cr.usgs.gov/data/atlas/little/.Accessed 2004 April 19.

Hart, J.H., and D.L. Hart. 2001. Interaction among cervids, fungi, and aspen in northwest Wyoming, p.197-205, Sustaining Aspen in Western Landscapes: Symposium Proceedings; 13-15 June 2000; Grand Junction, CO. USDA Forest Service Proceedings RMRS-P-18.

Madison, E., K. Oelrich, T. Rodhouse, and L. Garrett. 2003. Mammal Inventories, City of Rocks National Reserve. University of Idaho, Moscow, Idaho. 43 p.

McCool, S.F. 2001. Quaking aspen and the human experience: dimensions, issues, and challenges. Sustaining Aspen in Western Landscapes: Symposium Proceedings.. USDA Forest Service Proceedings RMRS-P-18, Grand Junction, CO, June 13-15, 2000: 147-160.

McDonough W.T. 1985. Sexual reproduction, seeds and seedlings. In N.V. DeByle and R.P. Winokus R.P., editors. Aspen: ecology and management in the western United States. USDA Forest Service General Technical Report RM- 119.

Miller, R.F., J.D. Bates, T.J. Svejcar, F.B. Pierson, and L.E. Eddleman. 2005. Biology, ecology and management of western juniper. Technical Bulletin 152, Oregon State University Agricultural Experiment Station, Corvallis, OR.

Mitton, B.J., and M.C. Grant. 1996. Genetic variation and the natural history of quaking aspen. BioScience 46:25-31.

Mueggler, W.F. 1989. Age distribution and reproduction of intermountain aspen stands. Western Journal of Applied Forestry 4:41-45.

Romme W.H. 1982. Fire and landscape diversity in subalpine forests of Yellowstone National Park. Ecological Monographs 52: 199-221.

Romme W.H., M.G. Turner, G.A. Tuskan, and R.A. Reed. 2005. Establishment, persistence, and growth of aspen (*Populus tremuloides*) seedlings in Yellowstone National Park. Ecology, 86:404-418.

Shepperd, W.D., D.L. Bartos, and S.A. Mata. 2001. Above-and below-ground effects of aspen clonal regeneration and succession to conifers. Canadian Journal of Forest Research, 31:739-745.

Shive, J. and C. Peterson. 2001. Herpetological Inventory of the City of Rocks National Reserve. Idaho State University, Pocatello, ID. 64 p.

Strand, E. K., and S. C. Bunting. 2009. Monitoring aspen in the Upper Columbia Basin Network: 2008 monitoring report for City of Rocks National Reserve and Craters of the Moon National Monument and Preserve. Natural Resource Technical Report NPS/UCBN/NRTR—2009/196. National Park Service, Fort Collins, CO.

Strand, E. K., S. C. Bunting, R. K. Steinhorst, L. K. Garrett, and G. H. Dicus. 2009. Upper Columbia Basin Network aspen monitoring protocol: Narrative version 1.0. Natural Resource Report NPS/UCBN/NRR—2009/147. National Park Service, Fort Collins, CO.

van Mantgem, P. J., and N.L. Stephenson, 2007. Apparent climatically-induced increase of mortality rates in a temperate forest. Ecology Letters 10: 909–916.

van Mantgem, P.J., N.L. Stephenson, J.C. Byrne, L.D., Daniels, J.F. Franklin, P.Z. Fulé, M.E. Harmon, A.J. Larson, J.M. Smith, A.H. Taylor, and T.T. Veblen. 2009. Widespread increase of tree mortality rates in the western United States. Science 323: 521-524.

Worrall, J.J., L. Egeland, T. Eager, R.A. Mask, E.W. Johnson, P.A. Kemp, and W.D. Shepperd. 2008. Rapid mortality of *Populus tremuloides* in southwestern Colorado, USA. Forest Ecology and Management 255:686-696.

Appendix A. Aspen stands in CIRO
(Including explanations of why some stands were not sampled)

Panel	Unit	StandID	Transects	Sample	Area (hectares)	WhyNotSample
0	1	1	0	No	0.5	Shrubby aspen
0	1	2	0	No	2.3	Shrubby aspen
0	1	3	0	No	0.6	Shrubby aspen
0	1	4	0	No	0.6	Shrubby aspen
2	1	5	2	Yes	2.0	
2	1	6	2	Yes	10.4	
0	1	8	0	No	3.6	Rocky and scattered stand
3	1	9	2	Yes	1.2	
3	1	73	1	Yes	0.4	
3	2	7	2	Yes	1.4	
3	2	11	2	Yes	2.1	
3	2	13	3	Yes	2.2	
0	2	14	0	No	1.8	Private
0	2	15	0	No	1.8	Private
0	3	16	0	No	0.6	Riparian
0	3	18	0	No	1.2	Riparian
0	3	20	0	No	0.4	Rocky ravine
0	3	21	0	No	0.6	Not much aspen
0	3	22	0	No	0.5	Ravine
0	3	23	0	No	1.8	Riparian
3	3	24	1	Yes	0.7	
0	3	26	0	No	0.8	Riparian
0	3	27	0	No	0.5	Riparian
0	4	58	0	No	0.8	Shrubby
0	4	59	0	No	0.3	Shrubby
0	4	60	0	No	0.5	Shrubby
2	4	61	1	Yes	0.6	
0	4	62	0	No	0.6	Shrubby
2	4	63	2	Yes	1.3	
0	4	64	0	No	0.4	Shrubby
2	5	30	1	Yes	0.4	
2	5	33	1	Yes	0.3	
2	5	37	1	Yes	0.8	
2	5	38	1	Yes	1.2	
2	5	40	2	Yes	0.7	
2	5	41	2	Yes	0.9	
2	5	42	3	Yes	2.1	

Appendix A. Aspen stands in CIRO (continued)
(Including explanations of why some stands were not sampled)

Panel	Unit	StandID	Transects	Sample	Area (hectares)	WhyNotSample
2	5	43	3	Yes	1.9	
2	5	45	1	Yes	1.1	
2	5	51	1	Yes	0.7	
2	5	52	1	Yes	0.4	
0	5	53	0	No	0.3	Riparian
0	6	28	0	No	1.9	Rocky transect not possible
0	6	31	0	No	4.0	Rocky transect not possible
0	6	32	0	No	1.0	Rocky transect not possible
0	6	36	0	No	0.4	Rocky transect not possible
0	6	39	0	No	0.6	Rocky transect not possible
0	6	44	0	No	0.4	Rocky transect not possible
0	6	47	0	No	1.0	Rocky transect not possible
0	6	48	0	No	0.9	Rocky transect not possible
0	6	49	0	No	0.8	Riparian
2	6	72	1	Yes	0.3	
3	7	50	1	Yes	0.4	
3	7	54	1	Yes	0.3	
0	7	55	0	No	1.5	Shrubby
3	7	56	1	Yes	0.7	
3	7	57	2	Yes	1.9	

NPS 003/105822, October 2010